1/08 0-4   LAD 10/06

RING OF TALL TREES

RING OF TALL TREES

John Dowd

Alaska Northwest Books™
Anchorage • Seattle

To Dylan and Olympia

Copyright © 1992 by John Dowd

Library of Congress Cataloging-in-Publication Data
Dowd, John.
    Ring of tall trees / John Dowd.
        p.   cm.
    Summary: Dylan and his Native American friends call on ancient
rituals and Raven the trickster for help in stopping a logging
company from clearing the old-growth forest near Dylan's farm.
    ISBN 0-88240-398-2
    [1. Old growth forests—Fiction.   2. Forests and forestry—
Fiction.   3. Indians of North America—Fiction.   4. Conservation of
natural resources—Fiction.]   I. Title.
PZ7.D7534R1   1992   92-19231
[Fic]—dc20   CIP
                                                          AC

Edited by Ellen Harkins Wheat
Cover and book design by Alice Merrill Brown
Cover illustration by Linda Holt Ayriss

Alaska Northwest Books™
A division of GTE Discovery Publications, Inc.
22026 20th Avenue S.E.
Bothell, WA 98021

Printed on acid-free, recycled paper in the United States of America

CONTENTS

1. Cedar Meadows Farm

Dylan jumped out of the old pickup truck and slammed the door. He ran around the front of the vehicle, unlatched the gate, and swung it open against the lush spring grass. With a crunch of gears, the loaded truck crawled forward into the puddle that had formed between the posts. His dad looked out the side window to where the muddy water streamed off the big wheels. Then he turned to Dylan and they both grinned.

They had arrived at their very own farm!

It was not a big farm to be sure—just fifty acres tucked up against the forest at the end of a gravel road, twenty miles from town. But it was good for 3,000 bales of hay a year, with plenty left over to feed a cow and a couple of horses. Dylan's father joked that they were urban refugees. He had quit the hectic city life of publishing deadlines and was determined to spend his time working the land. Dylan's mother would continue writing articles for magazines because she wasn't convinced that such a small piece of land could support their family. But to kids, a farm is a farm, and Dylan and his sister could hardly wait.

Dylan looked past the bleached cedar farm buildings to the wet, bright-green fields speckled with dandelions, and on to the somber old-growth forest that faded in layers up the valley. The rain had stopped, and ragged feathers of mist trailed from the treetops. He turned and watched the family station wagon surge forward, loaded low on its springs. His mother strained her chin over the wheel, while beside her, six-year-old Olympia bounced up and down on the seat with excitement. The car passed, pushing a muddy wave before it. Through a carefully measured opening in the rear window protruded the broad white head of his Great Pyrenees dog Banjo, his glistening black nose testing the air for new and delicious smells.

Dylan latched the gate and raced after the retreating vehicles. With a whoop, he leaped onto the rear bumper of the lurching station wagon and gripped the rope that secured the load on the roof. The car swung into the open farmyard and stopped alongside the pickup in front of the back door.

"You'll give me kittens doing things like that," said his mother, as she climbed out of the car. But she was smiling.

In the front of the truck, his dad was tearing into his briefcase and mumbling. "I'm sure I had it in here with the legal papers," he muttered.

Dylan's mother dipped into her purse. "Is this what you're looking for?" she said, as she handed him a key. "You left it in the real estate office."

The back door opened into a porch. Nails had been driven into the wall for hanging coats, and beneath them stood a rack designed for boots to dry upside down so water from the coats wouldn't drip into them. The handle of the kitchen door was worn smooth and had a dark halo of farm grime around it.

Inside, the kitchen looked enormous—far

bigger than the one they had had in the city. A massive woodstove decorated with blue and white enamel panels and large shiny nickel handles dominated the back wall. Beside it stood an ordinary-looking gas stove and a huge refrigerator with the door ajar.

Olympia went to the large window and looked out over the farmyard to the empty chicken coop and the old orchard that was bursting with pink and white blossoms. "When are we getting the chickens and the ducks, Mommy?"

"Just as soon as we settle in," said her mother.

The rest of the house seemed every bit as grand as the kitchen to the exploring children. They had seen it once with the real estate agent, but without the previous owner's furniture it looked twice the size and echoed with their voices. On the ground floor were four high-ceilinged rooms and a bathroom off a long hall. At the end of the hall stood a stained-glass front door and stairs that led up to two smaller rooms tucked under the slope of the roof. Each was instantly claimed by one of the children.

An indignant *Woof!* reminded them that they had left one of the family outside. Dylan ran to the car and opened the door. Out bounded the shaggy white bulk of Banjo. He did his little dance of glee to be free and then raced around the yard, nose to the ground, tail held high like an ostrich plume, and proceeded to claim the corners of all buildings as his own. He was just setting off to mark the rest of the farm and maybe the nearby forest as well when a sharp whistle from Dylan drew him back and he was given sentry duty in the kitchen.

Throughout the morning, they moved their belongings into the new house. A fire crackled cheerfully in the old woodstove, and in no time the room felt like home—especially when their old kitchen table was in place and laden with bowls of soup and toast.

After lunch, Dylan excused himself and slipped outside with Banjo. "Just going to have a look around," he said over his shoulder. Then, without waiting for a reply and the inevitable request that he should take his sister along, he hastened around the back of the barn and ran after Banjo down the field toward the forest.

2. The Old-Growth Forest

As they ran, sun broke through the clouds, lifting the gray veil off the forest so the trees towered green and beckoning. They reached the boundary fence together, and Banjo squeezed through the wire. He snuffled the long grass beside a shallow stream, then rolled and twisted his great torso in ecstasy before giving his mane a shake and plunging down the bank into a shallow pool. There he stood with the water cooling his belly while his long pink tongue slapped the surface noisily.

For a while Dylan walked alongside the fence, looking into the depths of the forest that crowded the opposite bank. It was a very old forest with large trees spaced well apart and a thin covering of undergrowth. At the corner of the field a stile invited him to cross. But forests can be scary places for a boy of ten, even if that boy has a big dog as a companion. He knew there were black bears around and had no wish to come face to face with one.

Glancing back, he could still see the barn and, at the top of the house, the two little dormer windows like frog's eyes looking over the rise of the hill. He had walked through the forest with his dad before they purchased the farm, but it felt much more spooky now that he was by himself. Yet something drew him toward the shadows ahead.

Banjo, as was his habit, was ranging wide, flashing through the undergrowth, returning every few minutes to check on his master. His ancestors once guarded the mountain passes between France and Spain. They had been bred to live and work on farms, and later were trained to guard the castles of French aristocrats. As puppies on French farms, Great Pyrenees traditionally were raised with lambs, which they were later trusted to defend against marauding bears and wolves. In Banjo's case the lambs were human, and all his life he had watched and worried over Dylan and Olympia. Woe betide any person or animal that threatened them with harm.

"Heel!" shouted Dylan, scrambling over the stile.

His sneakers were already drenched and scrubbed clean from the wet grass, so he splashed across the clear gravel stream and picked up the trail on the opposite bank. With his hand on Banjo's wet ruff, he entered the forest. It smelled of wet leaves and mold. The trail was wide and carpeted inches deep with damp needles that added a spring to his step and muffled the sound of his feet. He walked slowly with a firm grip on Banjo's collar. Frequently he glanced back over his shoulder where he could still see the bright green grass through the trees.

After a hundred yards or so, he paused and listened. Even Banjo held his breath. Somewhere far above, a squirrel chattered angrily. Then all was silence. He could hear his own heartbeat. The smell of tree gum hung heavily about him, mixed with the musky smell of damp dog fur. Looking back, he could no longer see the grass or hear the rush of running water in the stream. The silence felt like a heavy mist that flowed right through him.

The thick, tapered trunks of ancient trees reached through a high canopy of green toward the clouds. Some of the huge cedars bore long scars. He had learned at school that the Indians used to take bark from the living tree and weave it into mats and baskets. They used the trees but did not destroy the forests.

Sun filtered through in spots and played on the new leaves of spidery blueberry bushes that struggled to shake off the last signs of winter. Sodden moss grew deep beside the trail, softening the contours of a long fallen tree of gigantic proportions. Ferns sprouted along its length, unfurling delicate new fronds. Tiny white flowers on long stalks grew from stars of low, leathery leaves.

Relaxing, Dylan released his hold on Banjo's collar. The dog immediately trotted ahead along the path past a patch of old snow scalloped by spring rains and dusted with brown needles.

Dylan followed softly. In his mind he pictured an Indian padding these same paths a thousand years before, rushing to deliver an important message to his people. So he too began to run, and with this his fears faded. His was the world of the Indian runner. He felt free and strong. Up a small rise he flew, and through some young seedlings that whipped his face as he passed. Suddenly he burst into a clearing and stopped.

The glade was almost perfectly circular and was carpeted deeply in bright green moss with a scattering of huckleberry bushes at one end and a mound of moss in its center. Spaced evenly around the perimeter stood seven ancient cedars, each so broad that when he stood with his face against the rough bark, his arms outstretched, they felt like solid, wide walls. All were splintered and dead on their tops from old lightning strikes, but their bases were full and rounded, with dry rusty bark hanging like strips of brown cardboard. All bore old scars. Thick boughs bent out and upward from a point just below the splintered spires, each branch crested with a dark green tuft of foliage.

A pair of ravens flapped from one tree to another, cawing raucously.

"Hello, ravens," Dylan called softly. "You have a beautiful home."

The birds both settled on a snag, pointing their black beaks toward him, cocking their heads first this way and then that as if to gain a better view of the intruder below. How long he stood staring upward he could not say. The trees seemed to close in around him. He wanted to call Banjo but hesitated. He was reminded of a cathedral where his mother had once taken him to hear Christmas carols. Something told him he should not be yelling for his dog in this place.

For a moment he felt an urge to turn and run back as fast as he could, but the mound of moss in the middle of the clearing caught his attention. He edged toward it.

"An old campfire," he thought to himself.

The mound formed a circle just the right size. He was about to kick some moss away from one of the rocks when he had the distinct feeling he was being watched. His first thought was about bears, and he spun around, scanning the clearing. There, standing by the path he had followed, stood an old man holding a simple wooden staff.

"Hello," said Dylan, relieved. He thought he saw the old man nod. "Have you seen a big white dog?"

The old man looked at him, unsmiling. Then he shook his head ever so slightly and walked slowly into the clearing. To Dylan's amazement, he wore no shoes. A simple coarse-weave garment hung from his shoulders like a blanket.

"No dog came here," he said gently.

"Aren't you cold without shoes?" Dylan blurted out. He hadn't intended to say that.

The old man's wrinkled face rearranged itself into a grin.

"I don't need shoes," he said.

"That's what I say too but my mother doesn't agree. Do you live nearby?" asked Dylan.

"Ayee. . . . This is the land of my people," he said with a wave of his stick. "My name is Tamtlutna—Tree Watcher."

"You're lucky. It's a beautiful forest," said Dylan. "We have just moved onto Cedar Meadows farm."

The old man nodded thoughtfully but said nothing.

Dylan fidgeted with his feet and glanced at the entrance to the trail. "I guess I'd better go find my dog," he said, but the old man seemed not to hear him.

"So you like the forest," he said.

Dylan nodded.

"This is a special place," he said intently, as Dylan began to move toward the trail. "It is known as The Circle of Tall Trees, home of Raven. There is great power here."

A slow prickly shiver swept through the skin on Dylan's neck and arms. The two ravens above set up a clamor, and Dylan looked up to where others were circling above the trees.

The old man leaned heavily on his stick and lowered his voice to a hoarse whisper. "Raven warns of great danger. My people must hold or all shall be lost. But Raven, he will help. Use Raven." Then, turning, Tamtlutna walked slowly past the fire ring and across the clearing and disappeared into the foliage on the other side.

For a moment Dylan stood staring at the silent bushes. He glanced up again. The ravens had gone. A golden evening sun lit the treetops, warning that it was getting late. He turned and sprinted back down the path as fast as he could. Dizzy and breathless, he burst out of the forest, splashed through the stream, and scrambled over the stile. He didn't stop until he was halfway across the field. Then he remembered Banjo. He paused to catch his breath, and then put his fingers to his mouth and gave a shrill whistle. There was no friendly *woof* in response, and no sign of his dog as he neared the house.

A yellow truck was parked in the yard. COMOCO was painted on the door in blue letters.

On the porch, Dylan kicked off his wet sneakers without bothering to undo the laces. The sound of angry voices came from the kitchen. As he pushed open the door he heard a man gruffly say, "Well, that is the way it is. We have a letter from the previous owner giving us right of access and we mean to use it."

And he heard his dad reply, "I'm not the previous owner."

Dylan's father was standing at the kitchen table glaring angrily at two men. The smaller of the two had on a gray suit and held a thin leather folder in one hand. The other was big and bearded, with hands that were calloused and scratched like the bark of a tree. They brushed past Dylan as he walked in, and stormed out through the porch. His mother and sister frowned as the back door slammed.

"What was that all about ?" asked Dylan.

His father rubbed his eyes, and suddenly slammed the table with his fist.

"Hey," said Dylan. "Will someone tell me what's going on?"

His mother looked at him. "COMOCO is a Brazilian company that has recently bought timber rights throughout the province. They're planning to log the valley."

Dylan stared in disbelief. "You mean they're going to cut down the forest?" Tears flooded his eyes. "They can't do that. They've no right to do that."

"They say they have," said his father, grimly striding to the telephone. He took a business card from his pocket and stabbed the buttons of the telephone. His fingers drummed the table as he waited.

"Get me Mr. MacIntyre, please." He said "please" with difficulty. There was a pause. "I don't care if he is busy. Interrupt him. Tell him it's Mr. Jackson." And after a pause, Dylan's father boomed, "MacIntyre, why didn't you tell me they were planning to log this valley? . . . What do you mean I didn't ask? You know damn well we bought this place for the wilderness as much as anything else. They are talking about clear-cutting the whole valley. The whole valley!"

He slammed down the phone and went to the window. "Nothing is ever simple, is it?" he said, turning back to the family.

"We have to stop them," said Olympia.

"Yep. We'll have to fight this one," he replied.

3. THE RESERVATION

"Oh, have you seen Banjo?" Dylan asked, suddenly remembering what he had planned to say as soon as he got home.

"I thought he was with you," said his mother.

"He was. Then he took off just before I met the old man."

"Just what we need," said his dad, "a runaway dog." Then he wrinkled his brow. "What old man?"

Dylan told them of his adventures leading up to the disappearance of Banjo.

"That's funny. I didn't know anyone was living up there," said Dylan's father.

"Sounds spooky to me," said Olympia. "Ravens and things. I don't like ravens. They're too big and they kill other little birds. Did you see any bears?"

"Lots of them."

His mother looked at him sharply. "Be kind," she said.

Banjo had not returned by the time they finished supper. "Can we take the truck and go look for him? Please?" begged Dylan.

His father looked wearily at his watch. It had already been one busy day. He went outside and whistled loudly. No response. From one of the cardboard boxes in the living room Dylan's dad retrieved a hand-held searchlight and a coat.

"May I ride on the back?" Dylan asked.

"Me too! I want to come too!" cried Olympia.

"Then get your warm coats and boots on," he said, glancing at his wife.

"Not me," she said. "I think I'll stay here and unpack."

Dylan and his sister followed their father out and scrambled onto the back of the pickup. Their dad handed them the searchlight and ran the cable through the open cab window to the power outlet on the dashboard. "Treat it gently," he cautioned. "That's an expensive flashlight."

Dylan laid it down carefully on a folded tarpaulin, and the two children held on tightly to the rail at the back of the cab as the truck bounced up the drive. At the gate Dylan whistled and called again for his dog, without result.

A moment later they were on the road and headed toward town. Dylan picked up the light and flicked the switch. A bar of brilliant white light reached out from the truck and splashed color wherever it touched.

For almost five miles they followed the gravel road, as the white beam probed the clearings and flashed through the dark woods. Once the glowing green eyes of a pair of deer shone back from the edge of a stream as they crossed a narrow log bridge, but that and a coyote were the only signs of life they saw.

On the way back Dylan's father turned up an unmarked side road that ran through some scrubby forest. The road was wide and well maintained. After half a mile, they came upon an open swing gate and a sign warning PRIVATE ROAD,

TRESPASSERS WILL BE PROSECUTED—COMOCO FORESTS INC. If their dad saw the sign, the kids would never have guessed it because the motor didn't change a beat as they roared past.

Almost immediately they burst from the forest's dark confines. The truck skidded to a halt in the middle of the road. Dylan swept the beam of the searchlight down a hillside and across an opposite slope. For a moment he held the light on the twisted limbs and trunks of crushed trees. He could scarcely believe what he was seeing. Before them, not a tree was standing. The ground was covered with cut and broken trees.

"This is what they want to do to *our* forest?" said Dylan, incredulous.

"Yep. This is called clear-cutting," his father answered.

"We should tell the police," said Olympia. "They'll get the bad guys and put them in jail."

"I'm afraid it's not that simple," said her father. "The people who cut those trees aren't necessarily bad guys. They're just ordinary folks making a living."

"I wish they'd make a living doing something else," said Dylan, as he held the light on a huge log half buried in earth beside the road.

"Look. They don't even take all the trees. They just cut them and smash them!" Dylan's brain raced. "If the loggers aren't the bad guys, who are? The owners?"

"Not really," said his dad, "but they *are* a pretty insensitive lot. They just do their job and cut the trees the government says they can cut. And that brings money that the government needs as well as making them a profit. But it doesn't take the environment into account or the fact that they are cutting trees faster than they are replanting them."

"Then who are the bad guys?" asked Olympia in exasperation.

"Maybe it's us for letting them do it," said her dad.

"But I didn't even know people did this to forests."

"You do now," her father said.

They whistled and called in vain for Banjo, then turned the truck around and drove back to the main road. Before long they came upon another side road. This one was narrower, with a pile of gravel between the tire marks. It wound along beside the stream where they had spotted the two deer. A sign came into view: NO HUNTING— Sassqui Band Council. Soon the valley opened into fields and a cluster of simple wooden houses strung along the road with old cars parked at odd angles. Nobody could be seen though lights burned in most of the houses.

By this time the children were so cold they could hardly hold on to the rail. They banged on the roof and were just scrambling into the warm cab, when Dylan stopped, holding the door open.

"Sssh!" he said. "Turn off the engine, Dad." His father did and they all listened.

Woof! Woof!

There was no doubt about that bark. It seemed to come from a house near the far end of the village. They drew closer, turned off the engine again, and listened. This time the barking was continuous; Banjo had recognized the sound of the truck.

They all piled out. Dylan stood still, suddenly ill at ease. "Should we be here, Dad?" he asked.

"Sure. Just follow me," he said.

The children followed close behind as he headed up the path to the front door of a simple square house built up from the ground. A rusty snowmobile looked oddly out of place parked in the long grass. Light shone through the curtainless windows of the living room, and they could see the flicker of a television on the wall. Banjo's barking was interjected with his talking whine, now that he heard their voices. The sound came from a shed at the side of the house. Dylan's father knocked firmly.

To Dylan's surprise, the door was opened by an Indian boy about his own age. He wore jeans, a skateboard T-shirt, and high-top runners. He looked first at his dad and then at Dylan and his sister. When he heard they were looking for the white dog, he turned and called for his father. A lean athletic man with long black hair and clear brown skin emerged from the television room.

"So you're the folks with the big dog?" he said. "It chewed up nearly every dog in the village before we caught him. You're lucky no one shot him."

Dylan felt a surge of indignation, but before he could respond, his father said, "We've just moved to Cedar Meadows. He ran off on my son this afternoon."

"I was exploring the forest at the bottom of our property. While I was talking to Mr. Tamtlutna, Banjo wandered off."

The man looked sharply at Dylan.

"What do you know about Tamtlutna?" he said.

"He seemed to be a nice old man," said Dylan.

The man whispered something to the boy, who

left at a run. The back door slammed. When the man turned back to them, he seemed friendlier. "I've never seen such a dog fight in all my life," he said with a chuckle. "There was a bitch in season and a whole mob of local dogs chasing her. When your dog turned up the place went crazy. There must have been ten dogs fighting in the middle of town. He's nice, though. Gentle as a kitten with people."

"Is he hurt?" asked Dylan, anxiously.

"No, his coat is so thick nothing could get a hold of him." The man rolled his eyes at the memory. "Man, it was some fight."

At that moment, the boy entered with one of the band elders dressed in slippers and a bathrobe.

"These are the new people from Cedar Meadows," the man said to the old man. Then, turning to them, he said, "This is Grandfather. They call me Carl, and this is my son Jake. You better come in."

Dylan's dad introduced them all and someone switched off the television. Grandfather sat on the couch. Next moment, the front door opened, and in walked a short, powerful man with a mustache and a wool cap pulled over his ears. He tossed the cap onto the table and shook hands all round. He was introduced as Marshall, chief of the Sassqui band.

"So you're the new people from the hay farm," he observed. "It's quite a dog you've got there."

"Thank you," said Dylan, not sure whether it was a compliment.

Marshall turned to Dylan. "And you're the one who says he met Tamtlutna up the valley."

"Well, I did meet him," said Dylan, annoyed that they seemed to be doubting him.

"Where'd you see him?"

"In a clearing down in the forest near the ring of tall trees."

Marshall looked at the grandfather.

"What . . . uh . . . did he look like?" asked the grandfather slowly.

"Well, he was real old and friendly," said Dylan. "And he was carrying a walking stick. Oh, and he had no shoes on and only wore a sort of blanket. . . ." His voice trailed off as he realized suddenly that everyone was staring at him intently.

Choosing his words carefully, the grandfather asked, "What did he say?"

As best he could, Dylan repeated his conversation with the old man. When he finished, there was silence. Then everyone began to talk at once.

"What did he mean, danger? What sort of danger?"

"And what is it we're supposed to hold? And what does he mean 'use Raven'?"

"Maybe I have an answer to some of that," said Dylan's dad. "Today we were visited by two men from COMOCO. They said they were planning to log right up to the headwaters and needed access through my property."

"What?" snapped Marshall. "They can't do that while our land claim is before the courts."

"Seems they think they can. They said their permit predated the filing of your land claim. One of them was a sharp-looking lawyer."

A long howl ending in an impatient bark cut through the conversation. Dylan looked around in anguish.

"You'd better take these kids out to get their dog," said Carl.

Jake led the way out the back door with Dylan and Olympia in tow. He opened the door to the woodshed, and they were almost knocked off their feet when a great ball of wet, filthy fur barreled out and began to prance happily around them.

"Wish I had a dog like him," said Jake.

They walked Banjo over to the truck.

"Is he a hunting dog?" asked Jake.

"He chases rabbits, but he never catches them," said Dylan.

"He'd kill a wolf if he caught one, though," Olympia volunteered.

"Nah . . . he couldn't beat a wolf," said Jake.

"Sure he could. He was bred to kill wolves and bears. He's a Great Pyrenees," she argued.

"I have an air gun and my dad lets me use the .22," Jake announced.

"I've never been hunting," said Dylan.

"Indians can hunt whenever they want," said Jake proudly.

"Can I see your air gun?" Dylan asked.

Back inside the house the children found the four men seated around the table. They had been joined by a big woman with friendly wrinkles around her eyes. She greeted the children as they paraded through the living room to Jake's bedroom. From the closet, Jake retrieved a long air rifle which he threw to his shoulder.

"Pow!" he said.

"Holy cow!" gasped Dylan. "That's yours?"

"Yep," said Jake.

"My dad says people don't need to kill wild animals for food anymore."

"Maybe not in Vancouver, but here we live by hunting and fishing."

Dylan picked up the rifle and sighted along the barrel.

"Hold your hands like this," said Jake, moving Dylan's grip. "Keep both eyes open but just look through one."

The door opened and the large woman came into the room.

"Dylan," she said, "I'm Jake's mother, Maria. Would you come and tell us more about meeting Tamtlutna?"

Once again, Dylan repeated the details of his encounter in the woods. He couldn't understand why there was so much interest in the meeting.

"I don't know what he meant about the raven," said Dylan.

"Raven is the trickster," said Maria. "He is smart and gets his way through trickery."

"Maybe that's how we should fight the loggers," said Dylan. "But why not ask him? He lives nearby doesn't he?"

There was an awkward pause. "He used to . . ." said the grandfather, "but Tamtlutna died fifty years ago. He was buried with many of our ancestors down near the ring of tall trees."

Dylan felt a little dizzy. For a long time he could not think what to say. "You mean what I saw was a ghost?" he eventually asked, faintly.

"A spirit," corrected the grandfather. "He's the keeper of the forest. You're not the first person to have seen him, but you're the first he's spoken to. It's an honor. He was a good man who worked to preserve the old ways."

"There's no need to be afraid of him," said Maria. "They say he was very kind."

"Time we were leaving," Dylan's father said to everyone, suddenly looking at his watch. It was past ten o'clock. "I hope you'll keep me informed of what the council decides. Maybe I can be of some help. Oh yes, and thank you for taking care of our dog."

They left hurriedly and drove off into the darkness, the two children staring silently into the brightness of the headlights.

4. SETTLING IN

Olympia had fallen asleep by the time they arrived home. Her dad scooped her up in his arms and carried her straight upstairs, where she was tucked into bed with all her stuffed animals arranged around her.

When Dylan went to bed he asked that his light be left on. "Daddy, do you think that Tamtlutna is going to stop the loggers with tricks?"

"I think he was telling his people to."

"Was it really a ghost I saw?"

"I don't know. But if he's a ghost, he's a friendly one, so don't worry."

"Daddy . . ."

"Go to sleep now."

"Daddy . . . if they need to cut trees why don't they just cut the trees they can use instead of cutting everything and leaving most of it on the ground?"

Dylan's father stopped at the door, then returned and sat on the end of his son's bed. "They do sometimes," he said. "It is called hand-logging. But the big companies can't make as much money that way, so they like to clear-cut, burn the remains, and then they are supposed to plant new trees. They call it tree farming.

"The trouble is that they usually plant all the same type of trees, and nobody really knows whether that is going to be good or bad in sixty years' time. The old forests have a balance of different trees and plants. They are in harmony with the soil, the water, and the creatures that live there. You can think of the old-growth forests as libraries full of information we can hardly read. Soon we'll have no libraries left."

Dylan thought about that for a moment. "Can

the Indians read the forest?" he asked.

"Better than we can, that's for sure."

"I guess logging would upset the spirits too," said Dylan.

"Good night."

"Good night, Dad."

The next day was Sunday, and Dylan slept in until almost nine o'clock, when the smell of sizzling bacon drew him from the covers. Sunshine flooded his room. He went to the window and looked down the sloping fields to the stile, the forest, and beyond. He felt the new season sun warm his bare skin. He watched it twist spirals of steam from the cedar fence rails around the orchard and shine through the pink and white blossoms of the fruit trees.

A pair of ravens circled the cluster of tall snags that stood above the forest on the flats. To his right the valley formed a perfect U, filled with hazy shadow. The thought of that valley of old trees cut to the ground was unbearable. He pulled on his clothes and stumbled downstairs.

"My goodness, here is a sleepy one," said his mother.

Dylan gave her a hug and fronted up to the woodstove.

"Yesterday seems like a weird dream," he said, lifting the lid on a steaming pot. "Yuck! Porridge!"

"It's good for you," said his mother, scooping up the pot and pouring a generous portion into a bowl on the table.

"The old man looked so real. How could he have been a spirit?" asked Dylan.

"Who knows," said his mother. "There are many things we don't understand."

"I wish I knew more about it," said Dylan.

"Talk to Jake's grandfather. Maybe he could help you."

Dylan spent the day unpacking, and organizing his room. Monday would be his first day at the new school and his stomach ached at the thought. He and his sister would have to travel by school bus with kids they didn't know, kids who had been with the same classmates for years.

During the afternoon he helped his dad repair the paddock fence so they could keep a pony and a milk cow. They loaded hammers, an axe, a shovel, a chain saw, and a roll of wire into the pickup and drove to the back of the section where the previous owner had piled long, split cedar rails. Taking an end each, they carried the rails to the truck and laid them across the tray so they overhung each side.

Then Dylan climbed aboard the pile, and with Banjo trailing they ground up the hill in low-ratio, four-wheel drive.

A rail was dropped onto the grass wherever a replacement was needed. Dylan held each one as his father cut it to length. He loved the smell of the cedar that filled the air as the noisy little saw tore through the soft, red wood. And when the last rail was nailed into place and secured firmly with wire, they stood back and admired their handiwork.

"I think I am going to like living on a farm," said Dylan.

"Me too," said his father.

5. Nicholas

At eight o'clock the next morning, Dylan and his sister set off to wait for the school bus at the gate. Their mother came along to reassure them. When the big yellow and black bus arrived, they each gave her a lingering hug.

"Have a nice day," she said, kissing both children on the cheek.

"This is scarier than a forest full of ghosts," said Dylan.

"You'll be just fine when you get to school," she said unconvincingly.

The door swung open and the children climbed aboard. To Dylan's relief, the bus was empty.

"Hello! I'm Emma," said the lean blonde woman who sat behind the wheel. "Dylan and Olympia, isn't it? You'll always be first and last because you're at the end of the road."

They each chose window seats halfway down the bus. At the turnoff to the reservation, almost a dozen native children scrambled aboard, jostling their way to the back of the bus. They showed no surprise to see Dylan and his sister.

"How's your dog?" a familiar voice asked as they streamed past. Dylan looked around. It was Jake.

"Oh, he's fine," he said. "He slept a lot yesterday."

The bus rumbled on, picking up kids in ones and twos from the settlements along the road. Olympia moved in beside her brother as the seats around them filled up. Their new school, located on the outskirts of the town, was a low, modern building that took children up to grade six. They had been there once to meet the principal and their new teachers. Dylan thought it looked okay at the time. Right then he wanted to be almost anywhere else.

The bell was ringing when they arrived, so Dylan took his sister to her first-grade classroom. She hung back at the door, so he had to give her a gentle push. She looked back and for a moment he thought she was about to bolt, when the teacher put an arm around her shoulder and guided her to a seat.

Most of Dylan's fifth-grade class was already seated when he arrived. He looked around and saw no familiar faces except that of his teacher, Mr. Tennant, a slim man with a thin beard and glasses who smiled and motioned him toward a vacant desk near the window. Dylan went to his seat. He could feel the eyes of the other children on him as he stood taking the books from his bag and stacking them inside his desk. Hastily he flopped down on the hard seat, relieved to be lying low.

"Good morning, children," Mr. Tennant said. The babble of voices subsided to silence. "I would like you to welcome Dylan to our class. He has come to us from Vancouver and I expect you to make him feel at home."

A smothered giggle came from a group of girls near the back. Dylan felt himself turning red. He stared steadfastly at his empty notebook.

"Now would you please open your math book to page sixty." Dylan flipped through the pages. To his relief, he had already done the exercise at his previous school.

Dylan's teacher had cleverly seated him beside the most popular boy in the class, Nicholas. When they were filing out for recess, Nicholas cheerfully suggested that he could show Dylan around.

Dylan liked Nicholas immediately. He was a tall, athletic boy with a mop of sandy hair, and he wore the same brand of high-top sneakers Dylan had been bugging his parents for all year. Nicholas seemed at ease everywhere. He led Dylan through the corridors, past the office and the library, and out onto the playground.

"Do you play soccer?" Nicholas asked.

"A bit," said Dylan. He didn't want to boast that he had been one of the top scorers for the West Vancouver Selects.

"Great," said Nicholas. "This is Dylan," he called to the fifth and sixth graders. "He's playing on my team."

"What position do you play?" asked Nicholas.

"Center."

"Me too," he said. "But around here, kids

mostly just chase the ball."

The two boys joined the melee on the field. Within minutes, Dylan found the ball at his feet. Down the field he zigged and zagged, directing the ball with familiar ease. At least four boys tried to check him, but all were left standing, looking around for the ball. As he approached the crouched form of the goalie, Dylan tapped the ball across to Nicholas, who was running alongside. With a *whump* he booted it hard between the piles of jackets that formed the goalposts. Their team cheered.

"Hey, you're good," said Nicholas, enthusiastically. "You can play on my team anytime you want."

Each day Dylan joined the players on the soccer field. He scored several goals but also was careful to pass to other players. During one game, each goal his team made came from one of his assists.

Once as they were walking back to class from lunch break, Nicholas casually asked, "What does your dad do?"

"He works on the farm," said Dylan. "What about yours?"

"Oh, he works for COMOCO."

Dylan stopped in his tracks.

"You know. The logging company. He's the foreman," said Nicholas.

"You mean your father is a logger?"

"Yeah. Most of the kids' dads are loggers at this school. Hey! What's the matter?"

"Oh, nothing," said Dylan, recovering from his confusion and walking on with his friend. He could not have been more surprised if Nicholas had told him his dad was a werewolf.

Olympia spent her recesses and lunch breaks with Jennifer, a girl with long brown braids who lived in town. Jennifer's parents had given her a pony, which they stabled at a nearby riding school. Each weekend, Jennifer visited her pony and rode it with her instructor along the old logging roads.

"You should leave your pony at our farm," Olympia suggested. "Then we can ride together when I learn how."

On Thursday afternoons, Dylan's class spent an hour in the school library. He went straight to the section with books on Native American culture. There he found one on the mythology of the Pacific Northwest Coast Indians. It was a big book with black-and-white glossy pictures of ancient carvings and wild-looking masks.

One in particular caught his attention: the raven mask. Unruly "hair" made from strips of cedar bark topped an elaborately carved and painted head with a long, powerful beak. The eyes had little round holes drilled for pupils. For a long time Dylan stared at the page. It felt like those eyes were staring right into him.

"That's an unusual choice," said the librarian, when he came to check out the book. "Are you doing a project on Northwest Coast Indians?"

"No. I'm just interested," he said.

That night Dylan went to his room early and read until after the kitchen clock struck ten. What he discovered carried him back to an ancient time when the West Coast was inhabited solely by Indian nations. He read tales of fishing and hunting, of war, alliances and treachery, of elaborate ceremonies and great feasts, and of winters when the people starved.

He read the legends of bears that could speak, of battles with whales and great halibut, and about the spirits that inhabited the sea and the forest and the mountains. And he read about Raven, the mischief maker and provider of light—that master of disguises who lived on the fringe of human society and worked his will by means of cunning and trickery. When, at eleven o'clock, his mother came upstairs to see why his light was still on, she found him asleep with the big book open across his legs. From the page, the mask of the raven stared into the room.

6. THE RAVEN MASK

During the week, Dylan had occasionally spoken with Jake, but Jake had his own friends from the reserve, and though Dylan sometimes hung around hoping to be included, he always remained on the outside. It was Friday when an opportunity presented itself on the bus and he plucked up his courage. As Jake walked by, Dylan caught his eye.

"I'm going back to the circle of tall trees tomorrow morning," he said. "You want to come with me?"

Jake hesitated. "What for?" he asked.

"Maybe Tamtlutna will be there," said Dylan.

"That's not for kids, specially not white kids," said Jake, going to his seat.

Dylan bit his lip in disappointment.

Later, as Jake was leaving the bus, he paused by Dylan's seat.

"I'll come," he said. "But I have to be back in the afternoon. There's a meeting at my house and I have to look after the smaller kids."

"See you at nine," Dylan said. He was delighted. When they got off the bus, he raced Olympia down the driveway to the house.

Woof! Woof! Woof! Woof! barked Banjo. Dylan checked his watch. It was eight-thirty. He flung open the porch door just as Jake skidded to a halt on a battered BMX. Banjo danced around him in greeting.

"Finish your breakfast!" Dylan's father yelled from the kitchen.

Jake came in and sat by the stove while Dylan shoveled hash browns smothered with egg yolk into his mouth and gulped a glass of milk.

"You coming to the forest?" Dylan asked his sister, knowing he was safe.

"No way!" she said.

"What's the council meeting about?" Dylan's father asked Jake, as he stood watching another load of hash browns and eggs sizzling on the stove.

Jake said, "Something to do with the logging."

The boys left the house and set off running across the field toward the stile. Banjo raced ahead sniffing the ground, his tail curled high over his back. A heavy dew soon soaked their sneakers, but the mist was breaking up and a blue sky showed through in patches.

"My friends don't think Tamtlutna is for real," said Jake. "They say you just imagined it."

"Sometimes I wonder if I did," admitted Dylan.

"I believe you. Grandfather says he always knew Tamtlutna was watching the forest."

They climbed the stile and crossed the stream.

"Have you ever seen bears in these woods?" Dylan asked nonchalantly.

"Sometimes. The previous owner of Cedar Meadows shot a big black bear in the orchard last year," said Jake. "Don't worry about bears, though. They run when they hear you . . . usually."

This time Dylan kept Banjo at heel as they walked the forest trail. The blueberry bushes were noticeably greener, the ferns bigger.

"Look. This is bear sign," said Jake, turning over a clump of gray scat with the toe of his sneaker. "It's pretty old. Look. You can see where the bear tore apart that old snag over there." He pointed to what Dylan had assumed was just a crumbling tree.

"He eats wood?" said Dylan, greatly impressed.

"No, grubs and bugs and things."

"Oh!"

The two boys approached the thicket of seedlings that surrounded the clearing. Dylan noticed Banjo was holding back.

"Come here!" he said, in a firm but hushed voice. Banjo looked away guiltily and lay down.

"Come here!"

The dog turned his head. Dylan took a rope from his pocket and tied it to Banjo's collar. Together they could not make him budge.

"He's spooked," said Dylan.

Jake looked about him. "He can feel the spirits."

"Maybe we'd better go back," said Dylan.

"No. It's okay," said Jake. "Let's go on."

Dylan tied the rope to a stout sapling.

Carefully they pushed aside the branches and walked past the full bole of a gigantic cedar, then moved on into the clearing. It was exactly as Dylan remembered it. At least he had not dreamed that. A raucous *caw! caw!* from above told them the ravens had spotted them.

Dylan glanced quickly about him. "I wish they'd stop that noise."

With a parting screech, the birds flew off, leaving behind an eerie silence.

"What's this?" said Dylan, startled. "It wasn't here before." A stake had been driven into the ground close to the circle of mossy stones. As cautiously as if they were walking on ice, the boys advanced into the clearing. The stake was a little taller than they were. It was smooth and dark, and bound tightly near its top was a pair of black feathers.

For a moment, the boys stared wide-eyed into each other's faces, Dylan searching his friend's face for a clue.

"Let's get out of here," whispered Jake.

They bolted. Dylan paused just long enough to see the chewed end of the rope still attached to the young tree where he had left Banjo. Gasping for air, both boys catapulted over the stile and fell onto the grass together.

"Holy cow, that place gives me the creeps," said

Dylan. "Where'd that stick come from?"

"I dunno, but you could sure feel things there," said Jake, shaking himself.

When they rounded the barn, they found Banjo slinking away. "You ran away!" Dylan scolded.

The big dog bowed his head and then rolled onto his back.

All afternoon, the band council met at Jake's house to discuss what to do about the logging. Chief Marshall had telephoned COMOCO early in the week, but nobody would confirm or deny that the headwaters of the valley were about to be logged. He had called the Department of Indian Affairs, but no one there knew anything about logging in the valley. Also, the person they needed to speak with in the Department of Forestry was away for a week.

Meanwhile, rumors had reached them that access roads were to be started by COMOCO the very next week, so Chief Marshall phoned Dylan's dad that evening. The two men spoke for a long time.

When he eventually hung up, Dylan's dad looked pleased. "These guys mean business," he said. "They plan to blockade the road." He grabbed his jacket and stuffed some papers into his briefcase.

"I want to come too," said Dylan.

"You may have to wait in the truck."

"I want to come."

They were not the first to arrive at Jake's house. Several cars were parked outside, and people could be seen standing with their backs to the window. Jake opened the door and showed Dylan and his dad into a room packed with a dozen others.

Dylan noticed that he and his dad were the only people there who were not Indian. Then his eyes fell on a sturdy staff that lay on the table. Two black feathers were tied near one end and dirt stained the sharpened end.

"When I told Grandfather what we'd found, one of the men went to fetch it," explained Jake.

"Now you kids leave us to our meeting," said Jake's dad, ushering them out the door.

"Who put the stake in the forest?" asked Dylan.

"No one knows," said Jake. "Grandfather says the ring of tall trees is a place where strange things happen. In old times they called it "the circle of the raven" and they held healing and magic ceremonies there. He didn't seem surprised when I told him."

"I saw the mask of the raven in a book. It looked really spooky," said Dylan.

"Grandfather has a raven mask," said Jake.

"A real one?"

"Sure it's real. It used to belong to Tamtlutna. Grandfather promised it to me when I come of age."

"I bet that's what Tamtlutna meant by 'use Raven.' He was telling us to use the mask. Can we use it?"

Jake hesitated. "I'm not supposed to have it yet. Grandfather keeps it locked up, but I know where the key is."

Dylan followed Jake out the back door and across the garden to a woodshed at the back of the second house down the street.

"Some man from a museum back East wanted to buy it, but Grandfather refused. It's really old," whispered Jake.

Jake felt for a key under the step and, after groping with it for a few moments, opened the door. Both boys stepped inside and closed the door before Jake dared turn on his flashlight. Along one wall stood rows of neatly stacked firewood. Tools filled one corner, while the other was occupied by a cupboard with a substantial padlock.

"It's in here," he said, reaching for yet another key.

Jake opened the lock and swung wide the doors. Dylan jumped back as the beam of the flashlight fell upon the raven mask painted boldly in black, red, and white. It hung from a hook at the back of the cupboard, and the coarse bark hair cascaded down as if to give the beaked head a body.

"Let's get outta here," whispered Dylan, his skin creeping.

"Look! These are the drums," said Jake.

The light played on three tray-shaped skin drums that hung beside the mask. Each drum was painted with a pattern of red and black.

"Those are ravens too," said Jake, tapping one of the drums with his fingers. It made a sound like distant thunder.

"Let's go," said Dylan. "What if they catch us here?"

"They're all at the meeting," said Jake, carefully replacing the lock and clicking it closed.

Dylan did not relax until they were safely back in Jake's room. "How often does your grandfather use the mask?" asked Dylan.

"Almost never. Our people don't use the old things much."

"It's a great mask."

Jake shrugged. "It's powerful," he said. "It could make strong magic."

"You mean in the forest?" said Dylan.

"Maybe. If we wore the mask and lit a fire in the old rock circle, we might stop the loggers. We'd have to burn special leaves and do a traditional dance. Tamtlutna would approve."

"Do you know the dance?" asked Dylan.

"I've seen it."

"We could ask your grandfather. He'll know what to do."

"I'm not sure we should tell him till after we've done it."

"We could just borrow the mask and drums, then return them," said Dylan, feeling a touch guilty.

Jake thought about it.

7. GRANDFATHER

On Sunday morning, Dylan rose early. After breakfast he took his bike and rode back up the road to the reservation. Before he left, he took his dog into the empty hay barn.

"Sorry Banjo, but you have to stay behind. We can't have you getting into any more fights."

Banjo could not be consoled or bought off with hugs. He cried pitifully as he heard Dylan's bike gathering speed up the drive.

The road to the reservation was hillier than Dylan remembered. He was glad for the low gears and chunky tires of his mountain bike. For the first time, he noticed the big stumps amid the smaller trees that grew beside the road. Clearly the area had once been logged, and the forest he saw had all regenerated. He thought of the men who cut those trees, and wondered where all that wood was now. Probably their house was built from some of it. He was happy their house was built of solid wood, but sad about the big trees.

He turned off toward the reservation. The sky was a clear, pale blue, and sunshine touched the trees high up on the hillside. A bank of mist lay softly over the stream, flowing above the steaming waters and pouring beneath the bridge before dispersing in chaos when it hit the sun. Patches of frost-coated grass remained where the air lay still, and his wheels crunched through puddles crossed with fragile lines of ice. Dylan stopped to zip up his jacket, and tried to pull his sleeves over his freezing knuckles. Spiders' threads white with beads of dew sagged across his path as he rode on. He ducked what he could and wiped the rest from his face with his sleeve. He wondered how those threads got across the road.

The scent of wood smoke grew stronger as he approached the reservation, and soon the mist had a noticeably bluish tinge. As he rounded the final bend, the valley opened out and the yellow- and blue-painted houses stood brightly against the green hill all bathed in sunshine. Near the middle of town the longhouse glowed a rich cedar silver-brown. Steam rose from its shake roof.

A skinny, short-haired dog sounded the alarm and soon a network of dogs barked defiantly at the edges of their territories, maintaining a respectful stone's throw from the intruder.

Jake was sitting in the sun in front of his house with his bike in pieces laid out on the snowmobile. A couple of kids Dylan recognized from the bus were kicking a ball on the gravel road, while a rooster known to the boys as Mr. Cool stalked a meal in the long grass, keeping a wary eye on the soccer ball.

"What's the matter with your bike?" asked Dylan.

"I just put on a new tire," said Jake.

Dylan let his bike fall to the grass, and together they reassembled Jake's BMX. By the time they were finished, the sun was warm on their backs and steam rose all about them.

When the bike was ready, Dylan and Jake pedaled down the road to where two boys had set up rocks for goalposts. One of the boys was Jake's cousin Mike, a twelve-year-old with a mean "boot." He always kept one eye on Mr. Cool as they played. Then, just when the rooster seemed to relax, Mike would give the ball a mighty kick and the bird would squawk and streak away flapping, only to return in a few minutes to continue the game. Dylan had not seen the other boy before. His name was Sam, a ten-year-old visiting from the town of Terrace.

When the boys grew hungry, they raided the kitchen at Mike's place. Grandfather was in the vegetable garden breaking up the soil for planting. When he saw the children, he straightened his back, joint by creaking joint.

"Where's your big dog today?" he asked Dylan, looking around.

"I left him at home so he wouldn't get into any more fights."

The old man nodded. "That's good."

Dylan liked Jake's grandfather. He wanted to learn more about the ceremony of the raven but didn't know how to bring up the subject without giving away their plans.

Just then, a large raven landed on the peak of the shake roof and hopped along sideways, watching the old man with a beady black eye. "He wants me out of the way so he can get the worms," said Grandfather.

He broke one from the rich dark earth and tossed it wriggling onto the turf. The raven spread its wings, lifted into the air, and landed back on the ridge of the roof.

Grandfather chuckled. "Smart bird. He doesn't trust kids."

"You can't trick a trickster that easily," said Dylan, sensing an opening. After a short pause, he added, "Why do you call him 'the trickster,' anyway?"

Mike and Jake exchanged glances. Grandfather smiled.

"Ah, he's more than a trickster," the old man said. "He is a friendly spirit. They say he can turn himself into anything he wants—usually to make mischief."

"How do you get the raven spirit to make mischief?" asked Jake, innocently.

The old man looked at him sharply. "I'm not sure you need any help. Don't think I didn't see you boys kicking the ball at my rooster this morning."

"He likes to play ball with Mike," said Jake.

The old man nodded slowly and then fixed his gaze on the raven, which was hopping back and forth along the peak of the roof.

"You use the raven mask and the flat drums around the fire, don't you Grandfather?" said Jake, eager to keep the conversation on track.

Grandfather was no fool. He sensed he was being led on, but he could see no harm in it. It was seldom enough that the young people asked about the old ways.

"Yep. There is a special dance," he said. "You use the raven drum and beat it like, *BOOM! boom! boom! boom! BOOM! boom! boom! boom!* And the arms are held like this," he said, extending his arms like wings and bending his knees. He shuffled his feet and rocked his body forward and back and forward. "And when the fire is good and hot, you throw on green cedar boughs, and then the green needles of balsam fir. And the dancers move through the sweet smoke."

That afternoon, the field beside the longhouse was crowded with cars. Many of the band members who lived off the reserve had arrived to discuss the logging and work out a plan of action. Dylan noticed his dad's truck jammed in with all the others.

Longhouse meetings did not usually include outsiders, but Dylan's dad had agreed to help. He still had many contacts from his publishing days, and figured it was time to call on some of his old friends in the press. Besides, anyone trying to log the valley would want to cross Cedar Meadows first, so his cooperation was needed. At the front door, security men with red satin armbands greeted the visitors and ensured that those attending were known. The boys started a game of soccer on the street.

At the back of the longhouse, a door led to a kitchen with a counter that opened onto the main room. The tantalizing smell of cookies baking drifted through the open kitchen door and across the parking lot. Mr. Cool was pecking crumbs around the doorway and had completely forgotten about the soccer players when a sneak shot off Mike's mighty shoe brushed the rooster's tail feathers and hit against the wall like a runaway truck. Mr. Cool gave a squawk and shot into the kitchen. Yells and screams came from inside, followed by general uproar from the main meeting room. Mr. Cool exploded out the front door of the longhouse with a security man waving a coat in hot pursuit.

Three women stormed out of the kitchen. The boys, paralyzed with laughter, were too slow.

"Who kicked that ball?" roared Maria. "That was you Mike Mason, wasn't it? I'll have that ball."

Nobody messed with Maria. Not even Mike.

Dylan waited outside while the boys went into the kitchen to plead for their ball, but it was clearly a lost cause.

"Hey, come on in," Jake called to Dylan. "There's plates of cookies."

"Keep your thieving hands to yourselves," said a voice. Maria stood guard with a wooden spoon.

The boys crept in to the main room and sat under the open counter with their backs to the wall. It took a moment for Dylan's eyes to adjust to the dim light. In the middle of the room, a fire blazed in a circle of stone. Shafts of sunlight streamed through the smoke vents in the ceiling, illuminating huge blackened roof beams. Marshall and Jake's grandfather stood near the circle with blankets draped across their shoulders, and fifty or sixty people were arranged on terraced benches overlooking the fire. Seated on a chair was the band's lawyer, a tall bespectacled man complete with suit and briefcase.

"What are they doing?" whispered Dylan.

"They are calling the witnesses," said Jake.

"Calling what?"

"People are given a quarter to witness and remember what is said."

"Oh! That's not much money."

"It is just a token," said Jake. "It makes people listen better."

The calling of the witnesses seemed to take forever. Mike reached up and scooped some cookies from a plate, hastily rearranging the others to cover the gaps. The booty was passed along the row of boys.

When all the witnesses had been called and introduced, Grandfather led off, speaking first in his native Sassqui and then in English for the benefit of the few non-Indians and those who had never learned their native tongue. "We've been nice Indians too long," he rasped. "Enough is enough! Too long we have given and they have taken. Always we give and they take, leaving us with only the leftovers of what they have plundered. Soon there will be nothing left to give."

He paused and looked around the silent room. "Our riches are not held in banks. They cannot be measured by accountants. Our riches are the lands of our fathers and their fathers before them. Our riches are not measured in board feet or tons of pulp. Our riches are measured in living forests and clear waters. Our riches are our heritage and we are at grave risk of losing everything that is of value to us.

"For sixty years now we have been pressing our land claim, and still we wait and wait. Where has it gotten us to use the white man's system? Nowhere! The politicians nod to us and promise title to the land, which has been our homeland for thousands of years. Then they wink to their friends and let them in the side door to plunder the land. First they logged the lower valley. We did nothing, and now we inherit devastation. Now they want to log the rest of the valley. This time I say to you: Wake up! It is time for us to stand our ground."

Dylan listened intently. When the old man's words stopped, a murmur ran through the crowd. Grandfather turned slowly and fixed his audience with his fierce glare, then walked proudly to his seat. Other speakers followed, and everyone agreed the time had come to make a stand. Tamtlutna was never mentioned, but his presence hung like smoke in the longhouse.

The fourth speaker had just begun when Dylan heard a cry of pain from Mike. Maria's powerful hand was clamped around his wrist above the plate of cookies.

"Gotcha!" she whispered. "Now outside, all of you."

The boys scrambled out into the dazzling sunshine, but not before Jake had grabbed a pile of cookies, which they shared as they walked back up the road.

8. Friends at Odds

Dylan said goodbye to his friends, picked up his bike, and set off back to Cedar Meadows.

The afternoon sun was warm. The chilly world of that morning was transformed. Where once the ground was encrusted with frost and dew, vivid green grass had emerged, dotted with yellow, purple, and white wild flowers whose heads followed the sun's path across the blue sky. The young leaves on the alder bushes glowed a pale green. Dylan rode fast with his bike in high gear, savoring the wind that passed through his hair like fingers.

At home he found his mother and Olympia busy cleaning the old chicken coop. Clean straw was scattered around the floor of the enclosure. Stacked in wire cages outside clucked and cooed a dozen Rhode Island Red hens and a sturdy rooster with a bright red comb and feathers splashed with gold and blue-black. "This kind is pretty good at soccer," said Dylan, hastily withdrawing his finger from a sharp, jabbing beak.

One by one, the birds were released among the dandelion heads and new grass inside the wire run.

"They'll lay twelve eggs a day," said Olympia. "It's my job to feed them and collect the eggs."

"You're welcome to it," said Dylan.

The following day at school, Dylan was taking kicks at goal with his friend Nicholas when the ball ran close to a group of boys from the reservation.

"What are you playing with him for, Dylan? His dad works for COMOCO," called a voice from the crowd.

"Nothing wrong with logging," snapped

Nicholas, picking up the ball and hugging it to his chest. "My dad says if it wasn't for logging this town wouldn't exist."

"We'd be better off if it didn't exist," said Mike. "Who needs it?"

"Where would your folks get their welfare checks?" taunted Nicholas.

Mike burst from the group, fists clenched. A fight was averted only because at that moment a teacher walked up. "The bell has rung, boys. To your classrooms please."

"You'd think they owned the place," muttered Nicholas.

"They used to," said Dylan.

On the bus home that day, Dylan sat alone staring out the window as the noisy crowd gradually dwindled. It troubled him that two of his best friends had almost come to blows in the school yard. He felt torn. He had friends on both sides but belonged to neither.

Olympia plunked down beside him, and he realized the bus had stopped. "Well, are you coming or are you going to wait here until the morning?" she quipped.

He looked at the perky face of his little sister and felt better. The bus was empty.

9. The Blockade

"Looks like you have visitors," said Emma, as she turned the bus tightly at the end of the road.

Dylan peered out the other side of the bus into the mudcaked cogs and wheels of a huge bulldozer perched on the back of a flatbed truck. He leaped to the ground and was greeted by another gigantic truck with a slightly smaller bulldozer on it. A third truck with a large mobile trailer was parked near the gate to Cedar Meadows, and beyond that a couple of pickups and a fuel tanker were parked off the road. Around the gate stood half a dozen men. On the other side, his father barred their way, angry and determined.

The children pushed past the workmen. The gate was locked with a heavy chain and padlock, so they climbed over it and stood behind their father. The workmen had angry faces.

"Any person who enters this property will be charged with trespassing," said Dylan's dad.

"We have legal right of access to Crown land," said the big man Dylan remembered from the meeting in the kitchen the day of their arrival.

"That is Indian land, not Crown land," Dylan's dad said. "And if you think you are going to drive those things across my land, you'd better bring your slimy lawyer with you because you will need him."

The man was clearly uncertain what to do. He stood clenching and unclenching his fists. Abruptly, he turned and stormed off with his workers. They huddled for several minutes near the trailer, and then walked along the road and up the hill to the corner of Cedar Meadows, where the terrain was steep and thick second-growth forest crowded the fence.

The boundary there ran back down toward the

stream, plunging to low clearings of snow-flattened ferns and rushes. For a long time, the men stood pointing to the stands of forest on the flats below, then a number of them set off on foot, pushing through the scrub.

The family watched from the living room. Dylan's dad looked grim. He picked up the telephone.

"Marshall, this is Bill Jackson," he said. "They're here already . . . D8 and D6 Caterpillars and a trailer. . . . Yeah, I told them they couldn't cross, and that seemed to have stalled them for today. But now they're looking at the southwest corner. . . . No, I would have thought it was too steep, and the land at the bottom is pretty soft, but they might try it. . . . At any rate, I think it's too late for them to start work today. We could buy some time if the blockade went up during the night. . . . You're doing it already? Great. . . . That should give the lawyers time to do their thing. . . . Okay, I'll see you later."

The two children sat down at the kitchen table for a snack. Their father began punching the buttons on the phone once again.

"I do believe your father is enjoying himself," said Dylan's mother.

His dad paused and thought for a moment. "I guess you're right," he said with a grin. "So long as we're winning."

For the next half hour, Dylan heard smatterings of his dad's conversations with his friends in the press.

"Yep! The word is that the Sassqui are barricading the road east of the turnoff. Oh, and you might look at how COMOCO came by their permit. I smell a rat there."

When he had finished, he took the binoculars from a drawer and went into the front room. Dylan's mother and Olympia followed him. The phone rang and Dylan picked it up.

It was Jake. "We've got to do it tonight," he said. "Can you get away?"

"Sure. No problem."

"I'm bringing Mike and Sam. We have the drums and mask. Can you get an axe?" asked Jake.

"Yes. And you can eat here. . . . Just a minute." He put his hand over the telephone. "Mom, what's for supper?"

"Hamburgers," she called.

"Can I invite three friends?"

"Ask your dad. He's cooking tonight."

Dylan's parents were pleased he was making

friends so readily. He knew it would be a cinch if he asked just right.

"Okay with me," said his father.

"Yeah, that's fine," he said into the telephone. "See ya soon."

In the living room, the rest of the family was taking turns with the binoculars.

"They're going away," said Olympia, "but there is a man staying in the trailer."

Dylan watched the two pickup trucks depart, leaving the bulldozers like huge stranded crabs on their flatbeds. His dad started to cook supper, while his mother returned to the amber screen of her computer. Some time later, Dylan looked at his watch: 5:30. He knew it would be dark by eight.

"There are three kids with bikes climbing over the gate," announced Olympia.

10. Drums in the Forest

Banjo barked furiously as a knock sounded at the door. Jake, Mike, and Sam stood there, each carrying a hemp sack tied at the top and corners. They carefully put their burdens down in the porch and trooped into the kitchen.

"Great timing," said Dylan's dad, scooping up the sizzling brown patties and placing each carefully onto a buttered bun. "Help yourselves to ketchup and salad."

"Dad, we're going to muck around in the woods after supper," said Dylan.

"I want to come too," said Olympia.

"No way," said Dylan.

"Please."

"Forget it." Dylan's dad put down his spatula. "How about taking your sister?" he said.

From the next room, their mother called, "I don't like that idea. She's only six."

"I'm nearly seven," said Olympia.

"We're going to the ring of tall trees where there are bears, ravens, and ghosts, and we'll be beating drums in the dark. You would not want to be there," said Dylan.

Olympia hesitated for an instant. "I don't care. I want to go too," she said.

Dylan raised his arms in exasperation.

"I'm okay with your going if the boys agree to take you," said their dad, with a sidelong glance at his wife, who shrugged reluctantly from the doorway.

"We'll make sure she's okay," said Jake.

"Oh, goodie," said Olympia.

"Okay, but I'm not going to walk you home when you get spooked," said Dylan.

Olympia beamed triumphantly.

"You be back by nine," their mother said sternly.

The five children finished supper and raced out the door, pulling on their jackets and packs as they crossed the yard.

"Have you got matches?" Dylan asked.

"Yeah," said Jake.

Banjo tore around them in ever widening circles, brushing past the chicken coop and sending the startled hens flapping into the corner. From the toolshed, Dylan took a long-handled axe and a hatchet. Then, as an afterthought, he filled a bottle with paint thinner for fire starter and grabbed a flashlight from the truck.

In single file they crossed the field to the stile, splashed through the stream, and scrambled along the opposite bank to the blowdown cedars that had provided rails for the fences. The boys took turns lopping off branches and splitting the thick rings that lay about while Olympia stacked it neatly. Soon a huge heap of dry wood covered the path. They piled each other with armloads and set off for the ring of tall trees.

By the time they reached the clearing, the light was fading and Banjo had taken off. Mike took charge of lighting the fire. First he cleared the moss from the center of the circle of stones. He then lay a base of small dry branches and kindling. Around it he piled larger and larger branches and pieces of log until the heap reached almost to his waist. Meanwhile, the others returned to the fallen cedar and collected more loads of wood. They huddled close together as they returned, and nobody dared stop to pick up any pieces they dropped.

Darkness surrounded them by the time they dumped their burdens beside the fire circle. The bushes retreated to dark shadows. Far above, pale sky offset the black silhouette of the forest.

"We have enough wood to last all night," said Dylan.

"Let's light it," said Jake.

Mike poured the fire starter over the carefully built pyre. He struck a match and touched it to a piece of wood soaked with the fluid. Swiftly the flame spread upward, licking the kindling into blazing brands and driving back the darkness. Sparks rushed up to greet the first pale stars. The children crowded thankfully around the fire, soaking up the warmth. A golden light flickered on the trunks and branches of the tall trees.

"We forgot the green branches Grandfather said to use," said Dylan.

"I'll cut some if someone will help me carry them," said Mike.

The children looked at the dark shadows. No one spoke. Then Olympia volunteered, "I'll help."

Mike took the hatchet and Olympia the flashlight, while the others untied the sacks and carefully removed the mask and three drums with their striking sticks.

Mike and Olympia went to the fringe of the encroaching forest where cedar and fir saplings grew together. *Ping, ping* sang the hatchet as the lower limbs were chopped off and stacked in the clearing. Olympia scooped up a pile and staggered back to the fire.

Boom boom boom, Sam beat one of the drums. The noise was answered from above by an indignant squawk.

"We woke Mr. Raven," said Sam, peering at the treetops.

Jake and Dylan picked up the remaining drums and tapped them tentatively.

"Olympia. Your job will be to load the fire," said Dylan, tossing a green bough onto the blaze. Flame spurted from the resinous leaves, and a thick, yellowish smoke alive with sparks rushed up toward the ravens. Happy to have her own part in the ceremony, Olympia began breaking the greenery into smaller pieces and building a pile nearby.

With great care, Mike pulled the wood raven mask over his head and secured it with cords at the back. The three boys began to beat their drums in a chaotic rhythm.

"Wait!" cried Jake.

The drummers paused.

"Grandfather said to do it like this: *BOOM! boom! boom! boom! BOOM! boom! boom! boom!*"

"Don't hit those drums too hard," said a muffled voice from behind the mask. "We'll be in big trouble if one of them gets a hole in it."

Dylan, Jake, and Sam each sat cross-legged on one of the sacks, leaving Olympia perched atop the pile of cedar boughs. Wide eyed, she stared at the dramatic patterns on the mask. By the dancing light of the flames, she thought she saw the face move. Jake beat his drum faster, more urgently. The rhythm was taken up quickly by the others, and soon the forest throbbed with a deep, resonant sound—a heartbeat that linked them to the tall guardians of the circle—a sound that had not been heard in that forest for generations.

Raven bent deeply at the knees and began to stamp and swoop its wings. Olympia tossed more green foliage onto the glowing pyre and scurried back to watch. New flames sprang up and crackled through the greenery, and aromatic smoke billowed thickly.

As he danced, Mike gave little cries and yelps as if talking both sides of a conversation, as he had seen ceremonial dancers do at a potlatch. Around the fire he moved, crouched, arms outstretched, head down as if surveying the earth far below. Suddenly, with a screech that almost stopped the drummers, he threw his head back, and the light of the fire fell full on the wild colors of the mask. Olympia gave a cry of surprise as the face seemed to come alive with a wicked grin.

The hairs on Dylan's shoulders and neck began to prickle, and the sensation grew until it felt as if his skin were shrinking. *BOOM boom boom boom, BOOM boom boom boom.* He was no longer aware of wielding the striking stick or of holding the drum, or even of Sam and Jake sitting alongside. He knew only the throb of the drums and the wild, whirling vision of the raven in the glare of the flames.

Dylan's mind soared, and suddenly he was aloft, wing tip to wing tip with his friends, feathers rippling in the cool night breezes high above the forest. He looked down at the fire burning brightly in the clearing, its column of smoke rising through the old trees. To the west he spotted the line where the forest ended and the mangled remains of the clear-cut shone like bones in the starlight.

With an effort Dylan focused his mind's eye on the loggers and their machinery far below. He saw the chain saws with their ragged, toothy bars, and he saw the great tractors spinning and floating in space. He stared, unseeing, unblinking, into the bright orange coals, which burst sporadically into flame as Olympia tossed on more greenery. From the corner of his eye, he saw a shadowy figure with a staff, and a blanket draped across one shoulder, standing in the trees. But when he turned and looked, he saw only bushes.

Slowly the fire died to a glowing heap. The moss had been burned off the ring of stones, and smoke curled from the dried fringes. The drummers stopped.

"Put on some more wood," said Dylan.

"There *is* no more wood," Olympia answered.

"What happened to the big pile?" asked Jake.

"We've used it all." Dylan looked at his watch. "Holy smoke," he gasped. "It's after ten o'clock!"

Mike unfastened the mask and for a moment stared dazed at the remains of the fire. He felt strangely older than his years. He looked up. The stars seemed closer and more numerous than he had ever seen them before.

"Come on. We've got to get back," said Dylan tugging at his sleeve.

Carefully, Mike wrapped the cedar bark hair around the mask and slipped it into a sack while the others put their drums away. He watched as Dylan ground out the smouldering fringe of moss with his foot.

"You don't need to worry about it spreading," said Jake. "Everything is so wet around here."

The boys hoisted their sacks onto their backs, and Dylan collected the axe, hatchet, empty bottle, and flashlight.

"Let me carry the hatchet," said Olympia.

"Okay, but be careful."

Dylan turned the beam of the flashlight onto the trail and the group moved off, keeping close together. No one spoke as they padded through the dark forest. All eyes were fixed on the light dancing over the carpet of needles and undergrowth.

Olympia gripped the hatchet firmly in both her hands.

When they emerged with relief from the forest, there were lights in the field and voices coming toward them. Banjo burst out of the darkness with a suddenness that made Olympia yelp. Dylan embraced his dog.

"Where have you been?" he said. "Didn't you want to come with us?"

By this time, the search party was almost upon them.

"Is everyone all right?" called an anxious voice Dylan recognized as his dad's.

"We're fine. No problem."

"No problem! It's after ten, Dylan."

"Sorry, Dad. We lost track of time."

Marshall and Dylan's dad appeared out of the blackness.

"What have you kids been up to?" asked Marshall.

"We were down in the clearing," said Jake.

"So that was you with the drums," said Marshall.

The boys had not discussed what they would say if they were found out before they had a chance to return the mask and drums, and it hadn't occurred to them that they could be heard from the house.

"Yes," said Jake.

"No," said Mike, at the same moment.

"Well, what is it, yes or no?" Marshall asked. There was an awkward pause.

"Well, yes, some of us were beating drums, but no, it wasn't Mike," said Dylan.

"You've been scaring the hell out of the COMOCO watchman at the bulldozers," chuckled Marshall. Marshall told them how he had heard about the drums from a man who had overheard on the CB radio the frightened voice of the COMOCO watchman calling for reinforcements. He was expecting to be attacked by a horde of wild Indians.

"But you're going to have to explain to Grandfather what you've done."

"And you two," said Dylan and Olympia's dad, "you know better than to stay out this late. Tomorrow's a school day."

"Sorry, Dad," said Dylan. "We didn't realize it was so late."

Dylan's dad scrutinized each of their faces by the beam of his flashlight. "Let's get back to the house," he said.

Marshall left with the three boys. They walked slowly up the hill and climbed the gate, passing the boys' bikes over one at a time.

"Hey!" Marshall called to the men warming themselves around a fire in a fifty-gallon drum. "Just saw a band of Indians with bows and arrows sneaking through the forest."

There was no response. The boys laughed and tossed the bikes into the back of Marshall's truck. The engine roared, and soon they were winding their way through the night.

11. Banjo Triumphs

Dylan awoke suddenly the next morning. For a moment he could not remember where he was. He knew something important was happening that day, but the events of the previous night intruded like a dream he couldn't escape. With a jolt it came back to him that waiting at the gate of their new farm was a work crew and machinery preparing to destroy the forest. He threw back the blanket and scrambled into his sweat pants and T-shirt.

It was 7:15. Downstairs, his dad was pouring a cup of tea.

"What's happening?" Dylan asked, hovering his hands over the warm stove.

"The Sassqui have put up their blockade at the junction," he said. "They're not letting the work crews drive through."

"That means the school bus won't be able to pick us up," said Dylan, hopefully.

"They'll pick you up at the blockade."

"I'm going up to have a quick look," said Dylan, pulling his sneakers down from where they had been drying above the fire. Outside, he liberated the exuberant Banjo from the barn, swung onto his bike, and the two of them took off up the drive.

Dylan had forgotten about the gate being locked and he struggled to heave the bike over it, cursing the person who devised such an awkward shape for lifting. The watchman came to the door of his trailer to see what the noise was about. He paused for a moment, then walked over, lifted the bike easily off the crossbar of the gate, and set it on the road.

"There you are, young fella," he said. "That's a fine bike you have there."

Dylan looked at him in surprise. The man was tall, lean, and tough looking, but he was smiling in a perfectly friendly way. He wore a red and black wool shirt, blue jeans, and high leather boots with the laces flapping. Banjo, the fierce protector of the realm, came up, his tail wagging. He buried his nose in the man's crotch and in return had his ears scratched.

"Boy, that's a mighty big dog. I bet he could pull a sled all by himself."

"He weighs a hundred and fifty pounds," said Dylan, quite disconcerted that "the enemy" should be so nice.

"What's your name?" the man asked.

"Dylan."

"Like Matt Dillon?"

"No, like Dylan Thomas."

"How old are you, Dylan?"

"Ten."

"I have a boy who's just your age," he said. "His name's Nicholas."

"Nicholas?" said Dylan. "Nicholas Schroeder?"

"You know him?" he asked.

"He's one of my best friends at school," said Dylan, now utterly confused, his mind racing. "How come you want to cut all the forests?" he blurted.

The man looked steadily at him. "Forestry is my work, just like your dad's work is farming. We need the wood to build houses."

"My dad says the logs are just being shipped to Japan."

The man looked surprised. "That, I'm afraid, is too often true. It would be a lot better if they made things with the wood here in Canada."

"My dad says there'll be no old forests left in British Columbia by the time I grow up."

"I hope he's wrong," said the man earnestly.

At that moment a radio in the man's back pocket squawked.

"Tango Charlie, this is Roger Rabbit. Do you read me?" The man retrieved the radio and adjusted a knob.

"Who's Roger Rabbit?" asked Dylan.

"That's my crew. They're having a little trouble getting to work this morning." Then into the radio he said, "Roger Rabbit, this is Tango Charlie. I read you loud and clear."

"Tango Charlie, we can't get the vehicles past the blockade. The Sassqui have completely blocked the road. No traffic going either way."

"Can you get past on foot?"

"I'm not sure. So far they're only stopping vehicles."

"Then try and get the machine operators down here. I think we have everything we need already."

"Roger. This is Roger Rabbit out."

"They sound pretty funny on the radio," said Dylan. Then, "I'd better be going."

He climbed onto his bicycle. "Thanks for the help," he called. "Come on, Banjo."

The man waved the radio in farewell, and Dylan set off past the bulldozers and up the hill.

He was almost at the turnoff to the reservation when Banjo suddenly perked up his ears and began to prance forward, his tail curled over his back in anticipation. Rounding the final bend, they came upon a jumble of vehicles and a knot of people blocking the road.

"Heel!" shouted Dylan.

Banjo hesitated, and dropped back, loping along behind the bike.

The blockade consisted of a loaded gravel truck and a pickup parked end to end across the road. A narrow gap between the two vehicles was the only way to avoid climbing over the trucks or pushing through the thicket of blackberry bushes at either side. Dylan spotted Mike and Jake among those standing on the pile of gravel. Their grandfather, wrapped in a gray blanket, stood on the road with several other elders. Maria stood defiantly before the trucks with half a dozen other women, young and old. Sunshine bathed the whole scene in a bright light that belied the confrontation in progress.

About ten loggers, dressed for work, some with their lunch boxes in hand, stood face to face with a total of thirty or more Natives.

Marshall stood at the front, his solid frame blocking the way like a gate. "I told you already," he was saying in a firm voice. "There will be no logging of this valley while our land claim is before the courts."

Dylan leaned his bike against the tire of the gravel truck and climbed up beside Jake. "How long has this been going on?" asked Dylan.

"About ten minutes," said Jake.

All heads turned as a silver-gray Mercedes rounded the corner and drove up to the barricade. The loggers stood back as a large man climbed out of the back of the car. He was followed by two well-groomed German shepherds. The dogs obediently sat beside him and watched the crowd. When the man approached the barricade, the two dogs moved as one with him.

"Stand aside," he ordered. "This is a public road and these men have a legal right to go to work."

"Who gives you the right to cut trees on Sassqui land?" Marshall replied.

"We have legal right of access to Crown land," the man said. "It is *you* who are breaking the law with this blockade."

"No doubt, but those laws were made by the likes of you to protect your interests. You people seem to think that because there are trees, you have some god-given right to cut them. We don't recognize the law you speak of. This is Sassqui land, and the trees belong to the land. It has been a part of our people since long before the white man came. The Sassqui have never signed away the rights to this land."

The big man did not listen. He moved toward the gap between the two trucks. At some imperceptible signal, both of his dogs growled menacingly and moved quickly forward. Marshall involuntarily backed into the gap, and clubs appeared in the hands of half a dozen of the young men who stood behind him. The loggers moved in a ragged, uneasy line toward the barricade.

Suddenly a blur of white shot out from beneath

the truck and took the nearest German shepherd by the throat. In an instant, the dog was thrown howling onto its back. Banjo shook it from side to side like a toy. The second shepherd attacked, and, with a snarl, seized Banjo by the ruff. Banjo reared and stood momentarily on his hind legs as tall as a man, the first shepherd still locked in his jaws. The second dog hung on as he was lifted clear off the ground and tossed from side to side. Loggers and Natives stood back, aghast at the raw fury. Some teenagers on the barricade cheered Banjo on. The big man just stood by and watched confidently.

"Banjo!" screamed Dylan. "Come here!" Without a thought for his own safety he grabbed a sturdy stick, sprang off the truck, and with all his force laid it across the shoulders of the German shepherd fastened to Banjo's neck. The dog lost its grip.

In a flash, Banjo dropped the first dog and set his jaws around the other's throat, using his weight to throw it onto its back. Dylan was moving in for a second swipe, when the stick was wrenched out of his hand and a push from the big man sent him flying.

Nobody quite saw what happened next, but in an instant, Banjo had dropped the second shepherd, knocked the big man to the ground, and stood snarling on his chest, teeth inches from his throat.

Marshall helped Dylan to his feet. Both shepherds had scurried back to the car. The loggers dared not move.

"Get this animal off me. Get it off me," the big man pleaded.

Dylan put his hand on Banjo's chain collar. "Good dog."

At his touch, Banjo stepped off the chest of his master's attacker and followed him submissively back through the gap in the barricade. The big man scrambled to his feet and retreated to his car amid hoots and jeers from those on the barricade. The loggers milled about uncertainly. Then they, too, retreated and climbed aboard their battered crew truck.

12. The Cliff

At the blockade, Banjo was a surprised hero. People patted and praised him. Jammed between the links of his collar Jake found a broken tooth from one of the other dogs. The only injury Banjo suffered was a gouge on his snout.

"Thanks to Banjo, I don't think they'll try and break the barricade with dogs again," said Marshall.

At that moment Dylan's dad pulled up behind

the trucks in his pickup. Beside him sat Olympia wearing her school bag.

"You just missed a humungous dog fight," said Dylan.

"And you missed your breakfast," his dad retorted.

"Banjo attacked the manager of the logging company when he hit me."

"He hit you?"

"Well, pushed. Banjo knocked him down."

"What? How about starting from the beginning," said his startled father, handing Dylan his school bag. "There's an extra sandwich in here for your morning snack."

A crowd gathered, everyone talking at once.

"You should know better than to interfere with a dog fight," said Dylan's dad, when he heard the story.

"It wasn't fair. It was two against one," said Dylan.

"Well, neither of you seem any the worse for wear, and it is unlikely that the man will file any charges." He lifted Dylan's bike onto the pickup, locked Banjo in the cab, and went over to speak with Marshall.

"You need to get through?" asked Marshall.

"Nah. I just came up to lend a hand if it was needed."

"Seems your boy beat you to it," said Marshall, with a grin.

The big yellow school bus arrived and halted at the barrier. Dylan, Olympia, and the children from the reservation scrambled aboard, chattering excitedly. Dylan and Olympia sat at the back of the bus, with Jake and Mike soaking up the glory of Dylan's brief stardom.

"Your hands are shaking," Olympia observed.

"That's funny. I don't feel cold," said Dylan, gripping the back of the seat.

"What happened when you got home last night?" he asked his friends.

"Grandfather was pretty cool," said Mike. "All he wanted to know was if we treated the mask and drums with respect. He said he would have loaned them to us if we'd asked, and that it was a really powerful place to use them. He wanted to know what happened. He wasn't surprised we lost track of time like that."

At school, everyone had heard about the blockade. Some were in favor of it and some, mostly loggers' children, were against it. Few were indifferent, but many were confused. When Dylan saw Nicholas in the corridor, Nicholas turned and walked the other way. Dylan ran after him.

"Hey, Nick, I saw your dad this morning."

"Yeah, he told me on the CB."

"He's nice. He helped me with my bike."

"Yeah."

Dylan stood looking at his friend. "What's the matter?"

"My dad says the Mounties have been called. Someone was attacked there this morning."

"That was me. Then my dog knocked down the guy who did it."

Nicholas stared at him.

"We can still be friends," said Dylan.

"Yeah, you're right."

"You don't sound too sure."

"Well if your side wins, my dad won't have any work and we'll have to move."

"He might get another kind of job."

Nicholas pulled a face that said "fat chance."

It was a noisy ride home on the school bus that afternoon. A fight broke out between Mike and one of the loggers' kids, and Emma had to step in with a threat to make them both walk. The kids in favor of the blockade migrated to the back of the bus; the loggers' kids stayed near the front. Several children had a foot in both camps, and sat in the middle.

When the bus eventually arrived at the barricade with its remaining cargo, the first thing the children saw was a Royal Canadian Mounted Police cruiser, its blue and red lights flashing impatiently. Two officers lounged inside, their yellow-banded caps askew on the dashboard. Several city cars and station wagons were parked nearby: CBC TV was written on the door of one, CTV on another. A few trucks from the reservation were parked near the cruiser, but there was no sign of loggers. On the far side of the barricade, Dylan's dad waited in the pickup.

The crowd manning the barricade had dwindled to twenty or so people, including many non-Natives Dylan did not recognize who were mostly young except for one older, gray-haired couple wearing hooded duffle coats. Two men with television cameras on their shoulders filmed the children as they filed off the bus.

"Hello Dylan, hello Olympia," sounded a chorus of voices as they passed through the blockade.

Dylan hadn't felt so important since he scored the winning goal at the junior soccer playoffs last year. He grinned and gave a little wave. Olympia's heart swelled with pride as she followed her brother to the pickup.

"Hi Dad," said Dylan, sliding along the seat beside his father. "Who are the new people at the barrier?"

"They're environmentalists from Vancouver," he said.

"What's an environmentalist?" said Olympia.

Dylan said, "That's someone who protects the forests and the sea and the air."

Olympia shut the door and the truck began to move.

"Are we environmentalists, Daddy?" she asked.

"We're lazy ones who don't do anything till we're cornered," he replied.

Olympia frowned.

"Some of these people will be staying with us tonight," he added.

The truck rounded the final bend and started down the hill to the farm gate just in time for them to see the rear end of a big yellow bulldozer disappear into the bushes at the edge of their property.

"Damn! They must have walked through the

woods," muttered Dylan's father.

Several men were clearing away cables and chains and stowing them back on the now-empty flatbed trucks.

"You're going to regret this!" Dylan's dad yelled to Nicholas's dad. "That hillside is unstable."

"We've taken cats through steeper country than that," the foreman replied.

"No doubt. And what about the low ground?"

"Those drivers know what they're doing," said Schroeder. "I don't think they need our advice."

"You're not planning to drive those things up the salmon spawning stream are you?" asked Dylan's dad.

"I guess we'll have to since we don't have access through your property."

Dylan's dad shook his head grimly and drove on to the gate.

"Can you let us out here Dad?" asked Dylan.

"Sure, but stay on our side of the fence, understand?"

"Okay. We will."

While their dad drove down to the house to telephone the news to Marshall, the two children ran across the top field toward the snarl of powerful engines and the occasional puff of black smoke that rose above the young alders and birches on the hilltop. They watched in alarm as an alder close to the fence line toppled and fell. Then it seemed as if the forest floor itself were being rolled forward like a wave, as a huge bulldozer pushed its way toward the 200-foot cliff that dropped down to the flatlands by the stream.

As they neared the fence line, they spotted men among the trees. One was giving directions to the D8 driver. The smell of diesel fuel and exhaust fumes wafted over the green fields.

"Look!" said Olympia pointing up. Far above, two black specks turned and wheeled against a darkening sky.

"It's going to rain," said Dylan.

"No. There are the ravens," said Olympia impatiently.

"They're watching."

The D8 arrived at the edge of the slope and began to scoop out a hole twenty feet back from the cliff.

"What are they doing?" said Olympia.

"Making a swimming pool."

"Oh, smart."

The smaller D6 bulldozer lurched down the newly made track and drove almost to the edge of the precipice. There it stopped, and a man with a silver hard hat pulled steel cable from a drum behind the driver's seat. Meanwhile, the larger machine backed into the hole it had scooped.

"It has made a nest and it's going to lay an egg," pronounced Olympia with a giggle.

The man with the silver hat ran out some cable from the D8 and joined it to the end of the D6's cable with a shackle so big he needed two hands to carry it. Heavy drops of rain began to fall.

"Holy cow! They're going to lower one bull-dozer down the cliff with the other," exclaimed Dylan, eyes wide with amazement.

The children climbed the corner post for a better view. The man with the silver hat held up his hand and walked toward them.

"Quick, run!" said Olympia.

"No, wait. This is our property."

The man drew closer. "Well if it isn't the kid with the big dog," he said. His face was kindly. "That was quite a scrap you had with the boss this morning."

Dylan could tell that the man was not dis-pleased with the outcome.

"This is going to be very dangerous, and I want

you kids to promise me that you won't come any closer."

"Our dad already made us promise not to cross the fence," said Dylan.

"Good. Then I don't need to worry about you," the man said.

"Is the driver going to stay on the bulldozer as it goes down the cliff?" asked Dylan.

"Yep, and I tell you I'd rather it be him than me."

"Boy, he must be brave."

"Nuts, I'd say." He turned and walked back toward the two bulldozers as rain began to fall heavily.

The driver of the D6 tied a rope between the posts of his protective cage and adjusted it so he could run it under his arms while still reaching the levers. He wiped his hands on a rag that he stuck back into a box beside the seat.

Tightening the chin strap of his red safety helmet, he looked at the small crowd of work-men who stood watching, and then turned to his spotter—the man with the silver hat, positioned on the lip of the precipice. The spotter gave him the thumbs up through the veil of water streaming off the flat-topped roof of the D6.

The great motor roared at the driver's touch,

and black smoke drifted through the pouring rain. Already Dylan and Olympia were drenched, but they scarcely noticed the water pooling in their sneakers. Mesmerized, they watched as the tracks of the D6 slowly began to move and tension came onto the cable.

The bulldozer crept forward until the blade and half of the track overhung the cliff. The driver paused and slipped the rope across his chest and under his arms. He checked his chin strap and ran his tongue over his lips nervously. His hands fidgeted with the controls as if looking for a way to escape.

Then, ever so slowly, he rolled the drum winch, letting out cable an inch at a time, allowing the blade to tilt down until the machine hung forward from the cliff edge, almost vertically. And all the while the tracks ground at the crumbling cliff face, sending little avalanches of rock and mud cascading down to the flats below. The rain drove into the driver's face as he squinted intently at his spotter, who clung to a tree that commanded a clear view of both tractors.

The children scarcely breathed as the D6 bumped and jogged down the slope like a clumsy, yellow spider on a thread, sweeping away the small trees and bushes that had struggled to establish themselves there. The cable bit deeply into the soft, dark earth while the D8, secure in its increasingly muddy nest, shuddered with each movement of its companion.

"I've brought you some coats, but I may as well have saved myself the bother," said a voice.

Both children jumped and turned to see their father.

"Wow!" he said looking at the scene below. "They're sure determined. Look at that mud following him down."

Cascades of mud and rocks had begun tumbling down the scar created by the bulldozer. A heavy brown soup of muck piled against the drum winch, flowing over the tracks of the D6 and around the driver's seat.

"And it's a while since I have seen rain like this," he added.

Several minutes later, its cable fully extended, the D6 still hung a good fifty feet off flat ground. Dylan, Olympia, and their dad craned their necks from the fence top. Far below, the operator made a downward spiral motion with his hand. His spotter, who was now far out on an overhanging limb, relayed the message for the driver of the D8 to lower the D6.

Slowly, the winch on the D8 began to unwind and the smaller bulldozer descended out of sight. For what seemed like forever, the D8 roared and growled in its muddy nest. At last, a cheer went up from the spotter and the watchers on the clifftop. Those on the fence knew the D6 had reached flat ground, and they could not help but share the relief.

13. Mischief

Dylan, Olympia, and their dad climbed over the fence and gingerly approached the edge of the escarpment. Below them, the D6, uncoupled from its larger brother, was pushing its way through the marshland toward the river. Great chunks of mud fell from its tracks as it plowed into the soft ground.

The operator, realizing his machine was bogging down, hit the throttle. The engine crackled and the machine bucked and began to settle deeper, tracks flaying the mud. Frantically, the operator slammed the D6 into reverse, but it only settled further. Mud oozed over the tracks.

Quickly the operator reversed the winch. Then, springing out of the driver's seat, he grabbed the end of the cable and floundered to firmer ground, dragging it behind him. Still, the bulldozer settled lower into the ooze. And still the rain lashed down. Men scrambled from tree to tree down the steep bank to offer assistance.

Triumph had turned into disaster. The mud was up to the engine when the operator scrambled back and switched off the ignition. In the sudden silence, the mocking cry of a pair of ravens winging their way to the tall cedars startled those on the valley floor.

"The bastards are laughing at us," said Schroeder.

Dylan, Olympia, and their dad walked back to the house in the now fading light. Two small streams ran down the wheel tracks of the driveway, forming a temporary lake in the field near the barn. There, the newly arrived ducks were celebrating the improvement to the real estate, snapping up worms that had evacuated the flooded soil. A frantic whining and scratching came from the barn door.

"Has Banjo been locked up in the barn all day?" asked Dylan.

"You bet he has," said his father, levering off his gumboots at the back door.

Dylan unbolted the barn door and Banjo erupted joyfully into the yard, did a quick circuit that sent the ducks panicking across the field, then followed Dylan contentedly into the porch.

The kitchen was steamy hot. The rich smell of Irish stew emanated from a huge pot on the woodstove. Many of the environmentalists Dylan had seen at the barricade were seated around the kitchen table with mugs of hot tea and a pyramid of fresh muffins before them.

"Dry clothes!" their mother called, as Dylan and Olympia reached for chocolate chip muffins. The doorbell rang as the kids raced upstairs to change. More wet environmentalists straggled in with some reporters from the press.

A dozen media people crowded around the kitchen table that evening. Dylan and Olympia weaved in and out of the crowd, answering questions about their role that morning and what they had seen on the cliff during the afternoon. A photographer from the Vancouver *Sun* had Dylan pose with Banjo, and was delighted when the boy lifted the front paws of the abashed creature onto his shoulder, his head barely reaching Banjo's collar.

The new arrivals reported that the logging crew appeared mostly to have bunked down in the trailer, and a CB radio carried by one of the newcomers confirmed that the D6 was indeed firmly stuck in the swamp, and no attempt would be made to extract it until morning.

Marshall, Jake's father, and some other men from the reservation appeared at the door just as the children were being hustled off to bed.

"But tomorrow is Saturday," Dylan protested.

"That is why you've stayed up an extra hour," said his mother firmly.

The children lay in their beds listening to the rumble of conversation and the pounding of rain on the roof close to their heads.

The next morning, the rain had stopped. Fallen blossoms covered the ground like pink and white snow, and the new grass was beaten flat. The mud in the chicken coop was as smooth as tarmac, and the whole world looked clean and fresh. Blue sky showed through the gaps in the departing rain clouds. Olympia released the chickens and ducks to forage, and Dylan released Banjo.

"If that dog chases those ducks, it's the barn for him," warned his dad.

Dylan reined in Banjo, who was eyeing the ducks enthusiastically. Inside the house, bleary-eyed people were emerging from sleeping bags strewn all over the floor. Huge amounts of bacon sizzled in trays in the oven, while an assembly line prepared a mountain of buttered toast.

The telephone rang, and for a long time Dylan's dad stood at the kitchen window in intense conversation.

"Seems we can't apply for an injunction to prevent logging until Monday," he said, hanging up. "In the meantime they can begin cutting this weekend."

"If we camp in the woods they won't dare," said Julie, a student from Vancouver the children had immediately liked.

The others agreed. "They couldn't get an injunction to keep us out till Monday either," added Ray, a stocky fellow with red hair and a dark ginger beard.

At that moment, the CB radio crackled faintly. Ray grabbed it, fine-tuned the knob, and put it to his ear. Everyone waited quietly as a smile spread over his face.

"Someone sabotaged their saws," he whispered, putting the CB radio back onto the table. "It seems that all the chains have been removed from their chain saws."

There were hoots of laughter.

"But get this: they found them hanging from the electric power lines running to this house. They can't figure out how they got up there or how to get them down. It seems there were men sleeping in the trailer's tool room and nobody heard anyone touch the saws in the night."

"Who could have done it?" said an older man.

All around the room, people were shaking their heads.

"Must have been someone from the reservation," Julie suggested.

"Not likely. Not in pouring rain with live wires," said Dylan's dad. "And whoever did it would have to have worked on the saws in the dark in a room full of sleeping loggers."

"Whoever it was is one helluva trickster," said Ray.

14. Raven's Revenge

After breakfast the protesters set off across the field in the direction of the clifftop. Mike, Jake, and Sam arrived on bicycles, packs on their backs. "We're going to use the drums again," said Mike. "You wanna come?"

Dylan hesitated. "Yeah, but I want to see what they do with the bulldozers first. I'll meet you there soon."

The boys parted. Then Dylan called his dog,

and he, Banjo, and Olympia set off to catch up with the environmentalists and press at the corner of the field.

When they reached the boundary fence, they saw five men dragging a heavy, coiled cable along the newly gouged road. The D8 still squatted in its muddy hole, and a watermark around the engine showed that the cat had been almost submerged during the night's rain. Down in the flooded swamp, only the bright yellow engine cowling and protective cage of the D6 remained visible.

The men with the cable continued past some heckling protesters to the edge of the cliff. Two of them then went over the edge, dragging the cable, while three remained on the top holding an end to control its descent. The stiffly coiled cable managed to catch and hook up on every tree and rock in its path.

Then the drums began. *BOOM boom boom boom, BOOM boom boom boom.* The men on the slope stopped and looked at one another. It was difficult to locate the sound.

Schroeder looked over the tops of the trees, the tallest of which were almost level with the top of the cliff. Irritated, he wiped the mud and sweat from his forehead with the back of his leather glove. He and his companions then laid their backs to the reluctant cable and continued hauling it down the slope.

The men attached the new cable to the cable from the D8 and linked it to the one from the D6. Heavy shackles made the final connection, and the D8 engine crackled and roared to life at the top of the cliff. The protesters, who had been debating logging practices with the bulldozer operator, backed away from the huge machine as it sent chaotic little waves through the pool of muddy water.

The spotter positioned himself on a vantage point about thirty feet from the D8. From there he had a clear view of the bogged machine and the cable that joined the two bulldozers. Arranged along the clifftop, carefully beyond range of a whiplash cable, both loggers and protesters stood, their animosity shelved for the moment as they watched the drama.

On the opposite side of the bulldozer poised a camera crew, with tripod set and camera in position. Dylan and Olympia surveyed the scene from the safety of the top rails at their corner post.

Slowly, the D8 winch began to turn. The cable grew taut. Down in the swamp, the D6 refused to budge. The D8 operator looked quickly at his controls and back down along the rigid cable, as the motor revved and the cable bit deeper into the soft soil. Nothing gave. And still the winch drum continued to turn. The rear of the D8 sank lower and the drum winch shuddered with strain.

The D8 operator glanced at the tracks of his bulldozer. He noticed that the water around the tractor was suddenly draining away. "That's odd," he thought. Then he knew. He slammed the throttle closed and leaped off the huge machine. "Run!" screamed the spotter.

Frantically the D8 operator scrambled away from the crumbling slope. From the corner of his eye, he glimpsed his bulldozer sinking in slow motion past his feet. As the rear of the tractor caught on solid rock, it looped backward, its huge blade arching gracefully into space. He lunged forward and clamped his fingers firmly around the trunk of a small tree while, with a terrifying roar, the avalanche took away the slope beneath him. Then there was silence.

Below, the D8 lay upside down in a pile of earth and twisted trees, its tracks gleaming in the sun. Tangled cable lay about it like leftover spaghetti. Dazed loggers and protesters stood and stared.

Then, the sound of drums beating deep in the forest and the croak of a raven circling high overhead broke the silence.

Schroeder dragged his eyes away from the disaster below and went over to the D8 operator, who still clung to the tree. "You can let go of that now," he said, gently helping the man to solid ground.

Two RCMP officers arrived, picking their way carefully through the mud in their shiny black shoes.

"What's going on here?" said the first. He was a big man with a small trimmed mustache.

"Bit of a parking problem, officer," said the operator, smiling weakly.

The officers walked to the edge of the cliff and stood agog at the two half-buried bulldozers. They took pictures and asked questions.

Dylan, afraid that they might start asking about Banjo and the manager of COMOCO, took his dog by the collar and hurried back to the house.

The aroma of fresh baking wafted from the farmhouse. Dylan slipped into the kitchen and found trays of muffins cooling on the countertop. The sound of a vacuum cleaner came from down the hall. Quickly he scooped up half a dozen muffins and stuffed them in his shirt. Then, curled around his piping hot booty, he scurried down the field to the stile.

The stream was rushing along after the night's rain. Water swirled above his knees. Soon he was on the soft needle trail again, padding along, supporting his shirt with both arms so the muffins would not be crushed. Banjo followed. As he drew near the ring of tall trees, Banjo stopped and lay down.

"Stay!" said Dylan, realizing it was hopeless to try to make him follow.

The drums sounded louder and louder as he approached the clearing. An instant of panic seized him. Momentarily, he lost track of where and who he was. It was an eerie feeling, as if he were someone else watching. All sense of time vanished. He looked down and regarded his sneakers as if they were alien objects intruding between him and the cycle of living and dying trees—of ferns, moss, and tiny flowers that drew life from the bodies of dead giants. Then he burst through into the clearing. It was heavy with cedar smoke.

Jake and Sam stood beating the drums, while Mike danced with the raven mask before the fire.

Around and around he turned, his body rocking forward and back in rhythm with the drum beats. In the ground before them stood the feathered staff.

Dylan held up his hand. "You can stop."

The drums faltered and were silent. Mike tipped the mask onto his head like a hat.

"It's all over," said Dylan, handing out the muffins.

"What's all over?"

"All their machinery is wrecked. There was this humungous avalanche and the big bulldozer fell upside down on the flats by the other one."

"Yippee!" they shouted.

The boys threw the last of the wood onto the fire, and sat on the hemp sacks munching muffins and tossing sprigs of green cedar into the fire.

"Who did the saws?" asked Dylan.

His companions looked blank. "What saws?"

"Someone took the chains off all their chain saws and hung them over the electric wires to our house in the night. We thought it might have been someone from the reservation."

The boys shrugged. "Not that we heard," said Mike. "It couldn't have been done without turning off the electricity to the house, could it?"

"No. So who did it?" said Dylan.

A raven croaked high in the trees.

Carefully the boys packed the ceremonial drums and mask in their sacks. Leaving the staff as they had first found it, they filed out of the clearing and along the forest path back to the farm. Banjo greeted them at the barn.

"I told you to wait," said Dylan sternly.

Banjo rolled onto his back.

"It's hard to get mad at a dog like that," he sighed.

A pair of ravens watched them from the roof of the barn. One held a bunch of straw in its beak.

"Look, they're figuring on building a nest," said Jake.

"They see a supply of ducklings and chicks this spring," said Mike.

"You mean they would eat chicks?" said Dylan. He picked up a rock.

"Sure, if the mother isn't watching," said Jake.

Dylan hesitated, and dropped the rock. "I guess they can stay for now," he said. "And I'm not sure I want to start a fight with those guys anyway."

15. Summer

That evening, the loggers packed their remaining equipment and drove back to town. The Sassqui opened the barricade to let them through and cheered as the last truck passed.

On Monday, an injunction was granted by the provincial court, prohibiting any logging of the valley until the Sassqui land claim had been decided—a process that would drag on for another fifteen years.

COMOCO's insurance company had canceled their policy as soon as they learned the equipment had been taken beyond the blockade. For over a year, the bulldozers lay where they were, pending the outcome of court battles between COMOCO and its insurance company.

During the long, dry days of summer, the children from the reservation and Cedar Meadows spent many happy hours sitting at the controls of the bogged D6. Nicholas sometimes joined them. As for his dad, Mr. Schroeder—he started his own business planting trees.

About the Author

John Dowd has received wide recognition as the author of *Sea Kayaking: A Manual for Long Distance Touring* (1981), the "bible" of the sport. *Ring of Tall Trees* is his first book for young readers.

Born and raised in New Zealand, Dowd traveled throughout the world for fifteen years, working as a freelance writer and photographer, a diver in the North Sea, a safari tour operator in South America, and an Outward Bound instructor.

In 1980, he established Ecomarine, North America's first ocean kayaking specialty shop, in Vancouver, British Columbia. In 1984, he cofounded *Sea Kayaker*, the sport's first magazine. His articles on sea kayaking have appeared in numerous publications, including *Wooden Boat* and *Nautical Quarterly*.

In 1990, Dowd turned his energies to writing books full time. He is currently working on his second book for young readers, *Abalone Summer*, a thriller set in the Queen Charlotte Islands. He lives outside Vancouver, B.C., in a log cabin on a mountainside with his wife, his two children, and two Great Pyrenees dogs.

Readers of *Ring of Tall Trees* won't want to miss our other exciting books for young readers:

S'GANA, THE BLACK WHALE, by Sue Stauffacher.
S'gana is the compelling story of a boy's courageous struggle to free a killer whale from a marine park. Moved by his love for the beautiful orca (S'gana) and the human/spirit form in which she appears to him, the boy makes discoveries about himself and his Haida Indian past.
Hardbound, 224 pages, $15.95, ISBN 0-88240-396-6

THE WAR CANOE, by Jamie S. Bryson.
Mickey Church, a defiant Tlingit youth from Wrangell, Alaska, sees a vision of his proud Tlingit forebears and a fabled war canoe that changes his life.
Softbound, 198 pages, $9.95, ISBN 0-88240-368-0

ONCE UPON AN ESKIMO TIME, by Edna Wilder, with illustrations by Dorothy Mayhew.
Once Upon an Eskimo Time tells the story of a year in a young Eskimo girl's life at Rocky Point village on the Bering Sea Coast before the white man came. With 22 illustrations.
Softbound, 204 pages, $12.95, ISBN 0-88240-274-9

THE EYE OF THE CHANGER, by Muriel Ringstad, with illustrations by Donald Croly.
A tale of life on Puget Sound long ago, *The Eye of the Changer* tells of a Salish boy's ventures among the elements and the spirits. With 70 illustrations.
Softbound, 96 pages, $9.95, ISBN 0-88240-251-X

Ask for these books at your favorite bookstore, or contact Alaska Northwest Books™ for a complete catalog.

Alaska Northwest Books™
A division of GTE Discovery Publications, Inc.
P.O. Box 3007, Bothell, WA 98041-3007
1-800-343-4567